CW00349543

ASIANS IN BRITAIN

Acknowledgements

The photographs in this book have been taken over a period of twenty years.
Such a prolonged undertaking makes it impossible to thank everybody who has contributed,
but some individuals and organizations merit special thanks.

For work at the Bradford Heritage Recording Unit: Rob Perks, Olive Howarth,
Janet Godbold, and Donald Hyslop. Carol Greenwood, Steve Kerry, Caroline Krzesinska and
Mark Suggitt have also been very supportive of the Unit's work over many years.

For commissioning photography which resulted in many of the pictures included in this book:
Sean Williams and Brett Rogers at The British Council; Rory O'Connell at The Museum of London;
The Commonwealth Institute; Ajay Chhambra at The London Mela; staff at the Bradford Festival;
staff on the picture desk of The Guardian and Tony McGrath and Susie Foster at The Observer.

For help, advice and support: Irna Qureshi, Mumtaz Khan, Pete James and staff at
Birmingham Central Library, David Fitch and staff at the Bradford Interfaith Centre, Mohinder Chana
and family, Jasvinder Khosa, Shams Rehman, Catherine Rew, Kate Chatfield, Shah Nawaz,
Bashir Maan, Sara Assiz, Janet Assiz, Suki Patti, Manjit Kaur and family, Dinah Clark and Paul Johar.

For financial help with the accompanying exhibition: The People's History Museum, Manchester,
and Yorkshire Museums, Libraries and Archives Council.

For their work with the exhibition: Tony Parker and the BBC, Anjum Malik,
John Siddique, Monica Patel, Matt Doyle and Paul Thompson.

To my family, Elizabeth and Alexei, for love and support.

Finally my biggest thanks go to all those who allowed me to photograph them,
and were generous with their time, thoughts and hospitality.

First published in the UK in 2004 by Dewi Lewis Publishing, 8 Broomfield Road, Heaton Moor, Stockport SK4 4ND, England
Copyright ©2003 For the photographs, Tim Smith; for the introduction, Naseem Khan; for this edition, Dewi Lewis Publishing

ISBN: 1-904587-09-7

Design & artwork production, Dewi Lewis Publishing; Print, EBS Verona.

A project by Bradford Museums, Galleries and Heritage, part of Bradford Metropolitan District Council.

ASIANS IN BRITAIN

photographs by Tim Smith
introduced by Naseem Khan

Dewi Lewis Publishing

in association with

Bradford Heritage Recording Unit

Mosque reflected in the window of a fish and chip shop in Manningham, Bradford. 1996.

HOME GROUND

'Asians in Britain' is such a huge portmanteau term: it is hard to know how to unpack it. Look around you and you will see a vast disparity in religions, languages, lifestyles. This complex and extensive fabric slips through the fingers. On the one hand there's the glitziness of 'Bollywood Dreams', on the other the energy and grime of Brick Lane. There's the austerity of the mosques and the glorious elaborations of Leicester's Jain temple and the famous Neasden Swaminarayan Hindu Temple. There's the comfort of the well-heeled Gymkhana Club on the edges of Southall and the failing mills and unemployment of the north. How can you reconcile all these contradictions? The canvas of Asianness is too large for simplification.

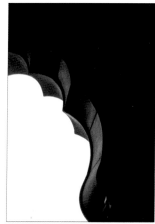

Entrance to the largest Sikh temple outside India, the Sri Guru Singh Sabha, opened in Southall, west London in 2003.

But it was not always so. I know this from my own life. Looking again and again at Tim Smith's images and the social shifts that they quietly mirror, I slowly realised that I had been witness to quite an extra-ordinary change, and one that rarely happens in society. In my own life time, the Asian community had grown and bifurcated. It had gone from being insignificant to substantial, from an aberration at the fringes to a major player and political force in virtually every town and city. It had made its way, in just fifty years, from the margins to the mainstream. How had this happened, I wondered? What had been my personal milestones?

Bidding farewell to relatives at Islamabad International Airport as they board a flight to Manchester.

There were, I concluded, certain moments when I consciously noticed that change had taken place and the landscape had dramatically altered. It is more than a matter of tangible landscapes: attitudes are even more important. When my father came to England in the 1930s, he brought with him the inevitable baggage of Empire. He had been to a Methodist-run high school in Central Province, before qualifying as a doctor at the famous Muslim university in Aligarh. But his ambition was to be a surgeon, and the West offered the pinnacle of training. In fact his dream was impossible – not that he failed his exams. But surgery at that time operated a quiet but firm closed shop, accessed only by upper-class white men. My small ebullient brown father in no way fitted the bill.

Like many immigrants of the time, he refused to let conditions limit him. He set out, with my mother – who had left Germany in 1934 – to earn enough to buy his first general practice. Where, did not matter. Chance took him to Birmingham – a city with a mere one hundred Indians on its rolls in 1939. It was here that they settled. In that vast post-war conurbation with its factories and workshops, our small Indian community – clustering together around the pioneering Indian Association – was hardly noticed. We were virtually invisible, and belonging to a minority in itself seemed a clandestine act. The monthly meetings of the Indian Association (in the days before Pakistan and Bangladesh emerged) took place for the most part secretively, in obscure hired halls in the back streets of Birmingham. When we left them at the end of our get-togethers, they appeared untouched.

Washing up in the langar (communal kitchen) an important feature of all Sikh temples, at Guru Tegh Bahadur Gurdwara, a converted clothing factory in Leicester.

Celebrating the Sikh festival of Baisakhi, at GuruTegh Bahadur Gurdwara. Leicester. 2002.

The mid 1950s brought the bombshell. Almost overnight the landscape changed. New immigration brought in growing numbers of people from the new India and Pakistan. They transformed the poorer streets of Balsall Heath – popularly called 'Little India'. Its grey hard-bitten Englishness acquired colour, noise, street life: and gave me my first encounter with a fully-fledged Asian society. I was enthralled. My father, on the other hand – and many of his doctor colleagues – was appalled. Overnight all their hard-won respectability with their stockbroker mock-Tudor houses, award-winning roses and public school children was put in jeopardy.

But the new wave did not care or maybe even notice, and in the end it was they that set the pattern. They grew the infrastructure that had been non-existent till then. (Buying spices had meant a trip up to London to Pataks.) Little by little, Asian shops arrived – cloth shops, groceries, travel agents. The new arrivals visited corner photographic studios and sent back brave portraits of themselves, consciously displaying badges of success – watches, fountain pens, brief cases. And my father unexpectedly discovered that the newcomers gave him back a quality of Indianness, because they perceived him to be an elder. His advice, as a professional man and a success, was solicited on everything from jobs to marital problems. And around him the community grew, absorbing him into the mosque committee that aimed to replace the shabby little mosques that had settled in back-street semis with a grand and obvious city centre edifice.

Religion led the way, but still culture lagged behind. When I was a child, I was crazy to learn to dance. All the little English girls at school were into tap and ballet, and their shiny dance shoes and little tutus seemed the ultimate in desirability. But dancing was a dreadful thing for a Muslim girl to do, so I grumpily retreated to Enid Blyton, and, as the years passed, things changed around me too. The 1970s brought culture into the frame. I stumbled on it accidentally through the unlikely medium of *The Times*. Ram Gopal, said a small advertisement, was opening a school for Indian classical dance.

Dance workshop organised by Aditi, the National Association for South Asian Dance, at a Hindu temple in Leeds. 1991.

I didn't realise the immensity of this insignificant ad at the time. Ram Gopal had been a name in pre and post war years when I was still deep in Blyton. He was the Nureyev of Indian dance. And his school was one of the very first to bring training in pure and marvellous classical dance to the British high street – if the Kings Road in exclusive Chelsea could be counted as High Street. Ram, by then in late middle age, was a glittering figure – vivid, sharp, unpredictable – and superbly gifted as a dancer. But like too many artistic talents, he had made his mark at a time when non-western art forms were pigeon-holed as dazzling visitors rather than welcome residents. A decade later and state funding could have nurtured him. But its patronage at that time reached out to the Western tradition and ignored the rest. Ram's school, with its top notch teachers, attracted around a dozen pupils, just under half Indian in origin, and went under after a year.

But local demand was ironically just about to take off. The Asian Music Circle – who first introduced Ravi Shankar and Ali Akbar Khan to the West – started their own classes five years later. And though they began in the modest front room of its director's family home, in no time the numbers had forced a move. As the 70s wound their way down, we trained exhaustively in the rigorous footwork, mime and codified moods of Bharat Natyam and – once we were thought to

Dancing to bhangra at one of the many Melas, or gatherings celebrating Asian culture, that have established themselves around the country over the past decade. 2002.

be good enough – sent out on the road as a touring company. Up and down Britain – Belfast, Bradford, Birmingham and more – we went, driven in a minibus by a shy giant whose dedication to the dance was total but whose sense of direction was terrible; so we frequently got lost. But our sense of the Asian community for whom we were dancing in festivals, cultural nights or religious occasions had no such vagueness. We were given a panorama of its strength and spirit, and lessons that were invaluable.

But then, after a year or so, something suddenly changed. We had been dancing for a community event somewhere in the Midlands. When we emerged from our dressing rooms afterwards, the hall had already been cleared and an activity that was unusual for the time was going on. In all our gigs, we had been used to traditional communities where the women and children had separated themselves off from the menfolk and a certain sobriety reigned. But here we were in a scene of immense hilarity. Young women and men were dancing and dancing together in a large circle, with the men rotating outside and clapping sticks with each young woman they passed. Everyone was having a very good time. Around the walls sat the elders, chatting away, with no sense of anything untoward or unrespectable taking place.

This must in fact have been one of the very first Navratri celebrations mounted by Asians who were in the process of being expelled from a number of East African countries. It was a ripple that turned into a wave that transformed cultural life, and economic life too. A 'second migration', they had already mastered the tactics of being both Indian and 'other'. They were, by and large, sophisticated and westernised and intensely entrepreneurial. The progress was amazing to watch. Officials from the little shop front that had housed the Bharatiya Vidya Bhavan – the institute of Indian culture – walked

Celebrating the festival of Navaratri at Shree Bhartiya Mandal, the Hindu temple serving the community in and around Ashton-under-Lyne near Manchester. 2002.

into an estate agents with an actual suitcase of money and came out as the owners of a vast church in West Kensington for their new cultural space. Around the country, music schools were being set up, temples and gurdwaras established, newspapers and radio stations started. Cultural centres were planned and a number of charitable voluntary associations – largely run by women – burgeoned. As we made our way around this new Britain, it was with wonder. These newcomers seemed fearless and ready to take on the world. That so many had arrived penniless was apparently – in their eyes – a blip, a temporary embarrassment that hard work and community backing would overcome. And indeed, so it proved.

How extraordinary then, that their coming gave rise to such fear and appalling hostility. New legislation was rushed through to remove their right to a British passport, leading to the sight of weary families being flown out to India and back to Britain and out to India again as neither side would give them shelter. Meanwhile right-wing politicians – using the platform established by Enoch Powell – made capital out of warning people of the dangers of thousands of aliens who would not, it was claimed, be able to assimilate into the British way of life.

Javaird Nawaz outside his shop in the Toxteth area of Liverpool. Set up by his father it originally supplied halal meat to ships with Muslim crews docking from South Asian countries. Liverpool, like many other busy ports such as London, Cardiff, Glasgow and Newcastle, became early centres of settlement for Asian men leaving the ships. 2003.

Looking today at some of the ventures that have brought Asianness into the mainstream, so many date from that immigration. The 'new maharajahs' feature in Claudia Cragg's book of the same name – kings of Tilda Rice, Meghraj Bank, Europa food stores; joined by young financial wizards and entrepreneurs, founders of the Asian City Club, upmarket leisure clubs and sports clubs.

So what is 'Asianness'? Where does it reside? Is there some special uniting quality? Hardly, examples show. In the eyes of much of the media, 'Asians' exist as an entity, but on the ground no such unity exists. Nevertheless, debate has ebbed and flowed since the 50s on the nature of proper policy around diversity, in some of which I have been actively involved. My work with the Arts Council explored the ways in which cultures meet, merge and evolve, and how a different kind of Britishness can develop and what that can mean. The role of the 'cultural navigator' has turned out to have extraordinary potential. Having to negotiate the rocks and rapids of differing expectations, customs, norms and forms, develops a kind of creative flexibility. The edges become blurred and porous. An Akram Khan can combine Indian classical Kathak with western contemporary dance, and emerge with a dance form that is seen as making a uniquely modern statement – a different sort of British.

The kind of combinations – in fashion, music and street style – that can co-exist blithely with familiar tradition would have confused and baffled my father's generation. But the confidence to play the system and to construct ones own multiple identity is a sign of ease and control. Tensions exist and inequality is still an issue, but nevertheless, visibility has come and defensiveness has vanished. In the High Court and the Stock Exchange, on the stage and in the streets, in television and multimedia and maybe even – or so I hope, for the sake of my long-gone father – in the operating theatre, Asians feature. In fifty short years, Britain has become home ground. It would, fifty years ago, have been unthinkable.

Naseem Khan
January 2004

A man from Oldham holds the medal awarded posthumously to his grandfather who was killed fighting for the British during the First World War. 2002.

Muslim burial plot at Brookwood military cemetery in Surrey.
India's contribution to the First World War was huge; an army
of over a million soldiers saw action in France, Belgium, Italy,
East Africa and the Middle East. 2003.

Member of the Sikh Ex-Servicemen's Association at a reunion in London. Some of those who fought in the First and Second World Wars settled here and provided the foundations for later migration. Other pioneers included sailors who, as part of the war effort, left their ships in the 1940s to work in munitions factories. 2000.

From the 1700s onwards the British Merchant Navy recruited large numbers of men from those areas of the Asian subcontinent that had a strong tradition of seafaring. Choudhry Qasim Ali (centre) tells his story of joining the British Merchant Navy and first sailing to London in 1921. He jumped ship in 1942. After setting up a fish and chip shop in Manchester he moved to Newcastle where his family now own a grocery shop, a take-away and a taxi business. 1997.

Shah Nawaz, who arrived in Britain in 1950, at the Camel Laird shipyard in Birkenhead where he worked as a welder for 27 years. He was one of the many men who arrived during and just after the Second World War, when Britain used the links established during days of Empire to satisfy a huge demand for labour. 2003.

Bashir Maan arrived in Glasgow in 1953 as a student. His command of English meant he spent most of his time helping other members of Scotland's fledgling Asian community. He went on to become the first Pakistani in the UK to be elected a local authority councillor, and among other notable achievements became Scotland's first Asian magistrate and District Court Judge. 2003.

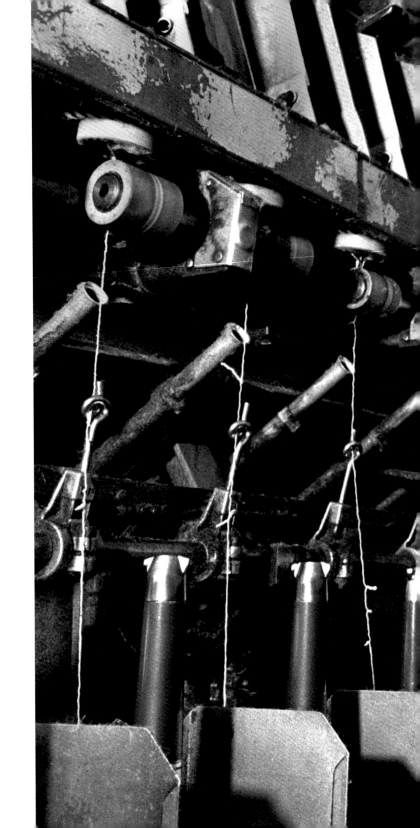

Doffing bobbins in a textile mill in Huddersfield. As the textile industry re-equipped during the 1950s and 1960s, firms needed to run the machinery twenty-four hours a day, and large numbers of Asian men came to work the night shift. 1996.

End of shift at the Vulcan foundry in Sheffield. 1984.

Spinning mules at work in a woollen mill in Huddersfield, one of the thousands of textile mills in northern England which first recruited Asian men during Britain's post-war boom. The family and village ties of these early migrants were often used to find new employees in later years, setting up a process of chain migration. 1996.

Woodhouse and Rixon forge in Sheffield, one of the many engineering firms of the Midlands and northern England which provided employment for early settlers. Much of it was hard and dirty work which was unpopular with local people. 1984.

Moving into a new house in the Manningham
area of Bradford, a typical inner city area
where early migrants would live in all male
households close to their place of work. 1992.

Pin-up in a spinning mill. Most men intended to stay as short term migrants, working
hard with minimum outlay in order to return to an improved life in their homelands.
However most eventually sent for their families, and the transients became settlers. 1987.

As women joined their husbands many of them found work in the clothing and textile industries. These women are spinning silk at Bingley Mills in Bingley, West Yorkshire. 1989.

The Sweet Centre on Lumb Lane in Bradford was one of the first cafes to open in the city, serving meals and acting as a social centre for men working the night shift in nearby textile mills. 1994.

Over the last three decades most of the jobs in traditional manufacturing industries have disappeared. This man works at Oxley Threads in Oldham, the only surviving company in the Manchester area to manufacture textiles from cotton. 2002.

Unemployed youths outside a snooker club in Swan Lane Mills, Bolton. At one time the town boasted over 120 textile mills producing yarn and cloth. The last of these, Shilo Spinners, closed in 2001. It operated from this mill, most of which is now empty. 2002.

A calendar in a staff room at Shilo Spinners marks the countdown to redundancy. Many of those who worked in the textile industry are now long-term unemployed. 2002.

Empty weaving shed at Lister's Mill in Manningham, Bradford. Once the largest factory in the world this huge building is now being re-developed for housing. 1993.

Preparing fabric for the manufacture of curtains at St Paul's Mill in Bolton.
Most of the employees in this factory used to work in the local textile industry
making yarns and fabrics which are now imported from abroad. 2002.

Making up curtains at St Paul's Mill in Bolton.
Most of the products are sold to catalogue
companies in the UK. 2002.

Making pikelets for supermarkets at the British Bakeries factory in Forest Gate. Many of the staff are drawn from east London's Asian communities. 1998.

A fabric shop in the centre of Dewsbury. With the collapse of employment in manufacturing many of those who had managed to save money used their capital to set up businesses that serve their own communities. 2002.

A girl waits for her mother to have her hair done at the
Tip to Toe Beauty Parlour in Longsight, Manchester. 2002.

Mr Tabassum is the owner of the Aakash,
listed in *The Guinness Book of Records* as
the largest Indian restaurant in the world.
It is housed in a converted chapel in
Cleckheaton, West Yorkshire. 2003.

Shimla Pinks in Birmingham is one of a new breed
of up-market Asian restaurants opening in cities
across Britain. 2001.

The police force is one of many organisations making efforts to improve the representation of ethnic minorities amongst its workforce. This recruitment officer is talking to young men at the Leicester Mela. 2002.

Filming a recruitment video on behalf of the Bradford and Bingley Building Society at its headquarters in Bingley, West Yorkshire. 1996.

Mrs Shama Ahmad who was Mayor of Newham during 1996-7. She was the first Asian woman in Britain to attain such a position. 1998.

Kiran Sirah at St. Mungo's Museum of Religious Life in Glasgow where he works in an educational role. He is studying Scottish sectarianism for his Masters degree. 2003.

The directors of Parsoli Finance, an investment company based in Dewsbury that specialises in financial advice that complies with Islamic beliefs. 2003.

Anjum Malik outside the Lowry Arts Centre in Manchester, where she was appointed as writer-in-residence during the Commonwealth Games. 2002.

Playing cards at The Indian Workers Association in Bradford. This organisation was originally set up in the 1930s to campaign in Britain for the independence of India, and as a mutual welfare society for those settling here. It was particularly active during the 1950s and 1960s, working on behalf of its members in the workplace. It now has an active role in providing services for the elderly. 1994.

The political life of the sub-continent is still very important for the older members of the community. Here Benazir Bhutto addresses a rally for the Pakistan People's Party at St George's Hall in Bradford. Early 1990s.

Advertising hoarding in the Great Horton area of Bradford. 1985.

An arrest after young men broke away from a peaceful demonstration in Bradford protesting against the publication of Salman Rushdie's *The Satanic Verses*. 1991

Disturbances in Bradford City Centre after the break-up of a peaceful rally calling for changes in the blasphemy laws following the publication of *The Satanic Verses* by Salman Rushdie. 1991.

Demonstrators in Trafalgar Square during protests in London against the looming war against Iraq. Over a million marchers made this the biggest demonstration in British history. 2003.

Young Muslims in Bradford protesting against the role of the West during the war in the Balkans. Late 1990s.

Banner protesting against Britain's blasphemy laws, during a demonstration in Bradford at the time of the publication of Salman Rushdie's *The Satanic Verses*. 1991

The Shah Jehan Mosque in Woking was the
first purpose built mosque in northern Europe.
It was constructed in 1889 to serve Muslim
students at a college nearby. The building
was designed by the Victorian architect WL
Chambers and mostly financed by the Begum
Shah Jehan, ruler of Bhopal State, India. 2003.

49

With the growth of the communities larger premises for worship were needed, and many buildings were converted such as this Wesleyan Methodist Chapel in Keighley, West Yorkshire. It was converted to the Shah Jalal Jame Mosque by the Bangladesh Islamic Association in the 1970s. 2003.

Worshippers leaving a church converted for use as a Sikh temple in Leith, the docklands area of Edinburgh. 2003.

With the advent of large scale migration in the 1950s many of the early places of worship were houses where men gathered to pray, such as this mosque established in the docklands area of Newport, Gwent. 1983.

The langar at the Guru Tegh Bahadur Gurdwara in Leicester. This communal kitchen where all visitors can share a meal, is an important feature of all Sikh gurdwaras. All the food is contributed by the congregation who take part in its preparation, serving and the washing up. 2002.

As well as catering for spiritual needs, places of worship also provide a focus for group activities and a sense of community. These women are peeling potatoes for a communal meal at the Guru Tegh Bahadur Gurdwara in Leicester. 2002.

Sikh temples are easily identified by the tall flagpole that marks each site. This is crowned by the Khunda, the symbol of Sikhism, which is taken down and washed with yoghurt as a mark of respect at significant festivals. This picture was taken during celebrations marking Guru Gobind Singh's birthday at the Ramgarhia Sikh Temple in Birmingham. 2002.

Receiving blessings at the festival marking Guru Gobind Singh's
birthday at the Ramgarhia Sikh Temple in Birmingham. 2002.

Getting ready for prayers at the Central
Mosque Ghamkol Sharif in the Small Heath
area of Birmingham. 2002.

Father and son at prayers, in a mosque
converted from a church in the Listerhills area
of Bradford. 1987.

Priest leading worship at the Sanatan Mandir in Leicester. This Hindu temple is a converted Methodist chapel, filled with Hindu deities and shrines carved from marble in India. 2001.

Israel Massey, a member of the Asian Christian Fellowship in Forest Gate, London. 1998.

Jemimah Prasadam, Anglican minister, at her church in the Lozells area of Birmingham. 2002.

Decorating a lorry with carnations at the Sri Dashmesh Sikh Temple in Lozells. This will carry the Guru Granth Sahib, the Sikh holy scriptures, through the streets of Birmingham during the celebration of the festival of Baisakhi. 2002.

The stairway to the main prayer hall at The Ghamkol Sharif Central Mosque which caters
for the largely Pakistani community of the Small Heath area of Birmingham. 2002.

Decorating a lorry with carnations at the Sri Dashmesh Sikh Temple in Lozells. This will carry the Guru Granth Sahib, the Sikh holy scriptures, through the streets of Birmingham during the celebration of the festival of Baisakhi. 2002.

Making a phone call during a Sikh religious gathering
in Handsworth Park, Birmingham. 2002.

Youngster at a ceremony to bless the laying of the foundation stone for a new Hindu temple in Bradford. 2002.

Leaving the supplementary school attached to Al-Hilal Community Project in Cheetham Hill, Manchester. This resource, attached to the mosque, provides a wide range of social, cultural, recreational and educational activities for the local community. 2001

Learning Gurmukhi, the script used by Sikhs for written Punjabi, at the
Saturday school run at the Guru Gobind Singh Gurdwara in Bradford. 1987.

Studying the Koran at a supplementary school
attached to a school in Bradford. 1987.

Offering prayers over the body of a Birmingham resident awaiting
transport to the airport before being flown to Pakistan for burial. 2002.

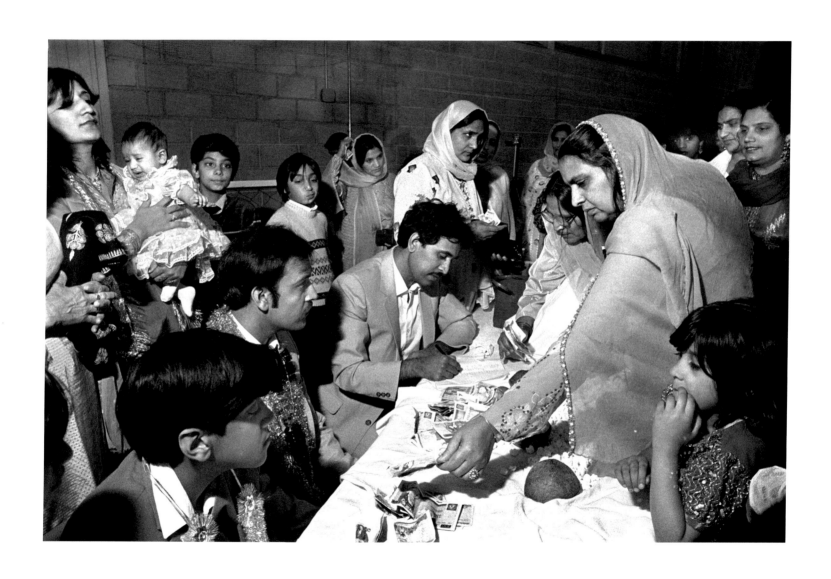

The night before his wedding guests offer gifts to the groom in the Newport Leisure Centre, Gwent. 1983.

Applying henna to the hands of a bride at her mendhi party
the night before her wedding in Bradford. 1996.

Performing a traditional stick dance at an all-women's party
the night before a Muslim wedding in Bradford. 1996.

As a sign of support a Muslim groom is fed sweets by friends and family at
a party the night before his wedding ceremony in Halifax. 2002.

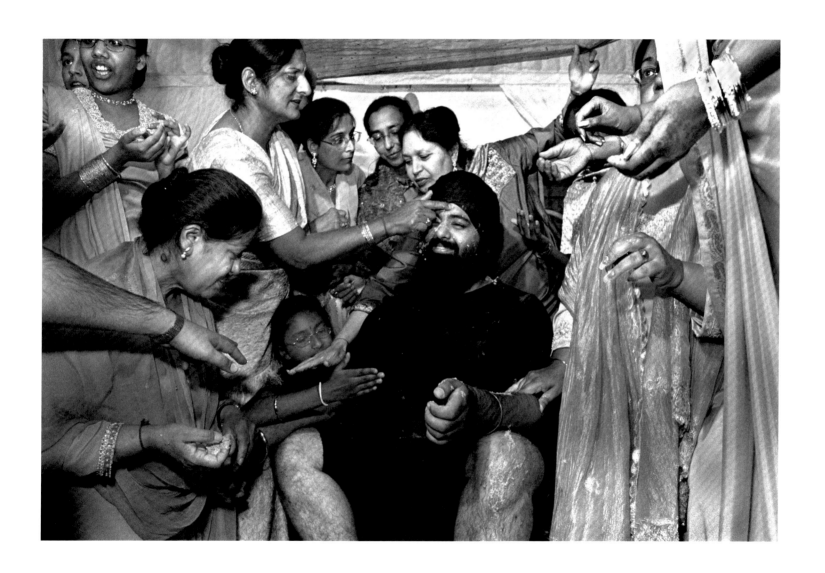

The women relatives of a Sikh groom wash him with mainya the night before his wedding. This light-hearted ceremony to cleanse the groom uses a mixture made of flour, mustard oil and tumeric. Bradford, 2002.

Final adjustments for the bride before the ceremony at the Shree Prajapati Hindu Temple in Bradford. The coconut held by the girl on the right symbolises how the marriage should be; strong on the outside and soft on the inside. 1987.

Bride setting off for her wedding from her
home in Girlington, Bradford. 1996.

Limousine collecting the groom from his home
above the family business in Bradford for his
wedding ceremony in Halifax. 2002.

As the families meet at a Hindu wedding near Huddersfield they compete to lift each other off the ground as a symbol of support in the years to come. 1986.

A Sikh bride and groom are congratulated by guests at the conclusion of their wedding ceremony in Huddersfield. 2002.

Guests gather for photographs at an Anglo-Indian
wedding in Patterdale, Cumbria. 1989.

Reception at the home of a Sikh bride
in east London. 1984.

Gathering in a Bradford household. 1996.

Social gathering at the British Asian Women's
Association in Forest Gate, London. 1998.

Braving winter weather in Bradford. 1992.

Last minute instructions before taking the
stage at the Leicester Mela. 2001.

Playground, Bradford. 1992.

Getting ready for a family outing at the home of
a Sikh family in Pudsey, West Yorkshire. 2001.

90

Family picnic on Wanstead Flats in east London. 2000.

Girls outside a function hall in Saltaire,
West Yorkshire. 2001.

Playing snooker in front of a mural depicting the journey from
rural Bangladesh to urban Bradford, at the Bangladeshi Youth
Organisation in the Manningham area of the city. 1990.

Purpose built mosques and temples are now a common feature of many inner city areas where the majority of the Asian communities live. This mosque caters for the large Muslim community in the Harehills area of Leeds. 2002.

Hanging out near the Wilmslow Road, Manchester. This famous road, known as 'The Curry Mile', is a busy centre for shops and restaurants. 2002.

Young men playing football in Oldham, 2001.

Saturday night on the Melton Road
in Leicester. 2001.

The Glassy Inn is a well-known Punjabi owned pub in Southall, West London. 2003.

Celebrations for Diwali and Halloween are advertised on Green Street in east London. 'Daytimers' are popular gatherings for young people who may find it difficult to go out in the evenings.1998.

Models backstage at a fashion show staged by Damini's, a well
known boutique on Green Street, east London. 2000.

Applying make-up to a model before a fashion
show in Manchester. 2002.

A cat-walk show held to celebrate the launch of Asian Fashion Magazine at Manchester Town Hall. 2002.

Audience at the launch of Asian Fashion
Magazine at Manchester Town Hall. 2002.

Supporters of the Pakistani cricket team at a match against
the West Indies at Bradford Park Avenue. 1993.

Supporter of the Pakistani cricket team.1993.

Celebrating the fall of the wicket of the England cricket captain,
Nasser Hussain, in a test match against India at Headingley in Leeds. 2002.

Father and son at a Sunday afternoon football match in Leicester. 2001.

Training session for the Morley Spurs Ladies Football Club. 2002.

Multi-cultural football tournament organised by the
Pakistani Community Centre in Oldham. 2002.

Watching a performance by a community
group at the Leicester Mela. 2001.

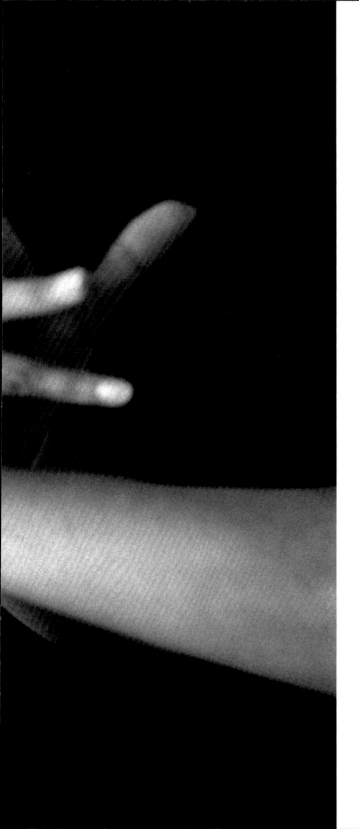

Dance workshop organised by Aditi, the
National Association for South Asian
Dance, at a Hindu temple in Leeds. 1991.

Picture This, a drama performed by Red Ladder Theatre Company in Leeds, features the story of a British born girl returning to India for the first time. 1997.

Audience at an amateur dramatics evening performance, in Bengali, of Agatha Christie's *The Mousetrap*, Scunthorpe. 2001.

Girls on a day out from the East End of London watch the making of a
Bollywood film, *Indian Babu*, in the shadow of Tower Bridge. 2002.

Bombay Dreams, the West End hit musical, at
the Apollo Theatre in Victoria, London. 2002.

Bollywood superstars Rani Mukherjee, Hrithik Roshan and Kareena Kapoor perform a song and dance routine during the making of the blockbuster *Mujhse Dosti Karoge* in The Lake District. This romantic comedy was shot in India, and in Britain where Hrithik Roshan's character lives. 2002.

Jaz Phandar, from Essex, being made up for a scene being shot in the City of London for the film *Indian Babu*, produced by his father. The film takes place in both England and India and he hopes it will lead to him becoming the first non-resident Indian to become a Bollywood star. 2002.

This reception at Watermans Art Centre for an exhibition of Bollywood film posters featured a special guest, the Madame Tussaud's waxwork model of Bollywood star Amitabh Bachan. 2002.

Enjoying a ride at the Bradford Mela. 1994

Meeting an old friend at the West Indian
Carnival in Chapeltown, Leeds. 2002.

Pakistan's biggest celebration is the spring kite festival
of Basant, held in Lahore. This tradition has now been
brought to Britain. These boys are holding Pakistani fighting
kites at Bradford's first Lahori style kite festival. 2003.

A performing Yorkshireman Steam Engine at the
Bradford Mela. Over the past fifteen years this event has
grown from a modest stage erected on a football pitch
to an annual gathering that attracts over 100,000 people
for a weekend of celebration of Asian culture. 1991.

Crowd in front of a music stage at the Manchester Mela. Most cities in Britain with a significant Asian community now stage their own Mela. The word comes from the Sanskrit, and is commonly used to describe a large gathering of people celebrating artistic, religious or political events. 2002.

Couple at the Edinburgh Mela in front of a hoarding for the Bollywood classic *Mother India*. This epic tale of a woman and her life of love and sorrow in a small farming community became one of the most famous Hindi films ever made, but is very different to the racy, fast-cutting, up-beat, MTV-influenced Bollywood films of today. 2003.

DELECIUS AND TASTY LAHORI

KULFI

قلفی

INGREDIENTS
PISTACHIO CARDAMON
MILK SUGAR
ALMOND

عمدہ ولذیذ
پستہ بادام
کھویا الائچی سے
تیار کردہ

پیشکش

میاں لاہوری

لاہوری

PRICE 1£2

قیت ۱ و ۲ پونڈ

Advertising 'Lahori ice cream' at the
Leicester Mela during the summer
of the football World Cup. 2002.

Graduation day at the University of Bradford. 2001.